# SPERANZA

## MUSINGS OF THE HEART

RAISUN MATHEW

Made with ♥ on the Notion Press Platform
www.notionpress.com

*

2022-2026
Computer Science and Engineering - Data Science

Jain (Deemed-to-be University)
Bangalore, Karnataka, India

*

# Contents

*Preface* *vii*

*Acknowledgements* *ix*

1. Fights 1
2. The Green War 2
3. Mused In Thoughts 4
4. In Love 5
5. The Blue Sky 6
6. Verdant Nature 7
7. One Heart 8
8. The Passing Time 9
9. Sunlight 10
10. Sleepless Nights 11
11. The Edge Of Seventeen 12
12. I Wish I Was Still Five 14
13. Our Nature 15
14. It Takes Courage To Be A Coward 16
15. The Kid 18
16. As Long As You Love 19
17. Glimpse Of Youth 20
18. Sad Truth 21
19. Secret Crush 22
20. In My Head 23
21. The Dark 24
22. Guess Me 25
23. Unfair 26
24. Rain! Oh Mighty Rain 27

# Contents

25. Rise 28

26. Dear Brother 29

27. Mobile Phone 30

28. Trip To Ooty 31

29. The Mirror 32

30. Magnificent Mother Nature 33

31. The Search For A Cloud 34

32. The Unforgiving Passage Of Time 35

33. To My Mother 36

34. First Love 37

35. Her 38

36. The Lipstick On Lips 39

37. Friendship For Life 40

38. The Moon 41

39. The Root Of Life 42

40. The Joy Of Life 43

41. The Cricket World 44

42. Untangling Depression 45

43. Playground 46

44. Violet's Mystery 47

45. The Darkest Days 49

46. Flower 50

47. Worth Of Failure 51

48. The Red Rose 52

49. In The Streets Of Lahore 53

50. I Shall 55

# Preface

'Speranza' is a beacon of light in the midst of darkness. It whispers to us that no matter how dire our circumstances may seem, things will get better. It gives us the courage to keep moving forward, even when we cannot see the end in sight. Its warm embrace lifts us up when we are feeling down and helps us find strength when we are feeling weak. I believe that life in the present world that is haunted by many circumstances require hope at its best to overcome the many challenges.

It is with great honor and privilege that I present to you this edited poetry collection, crafted by the group of talented and dedicated engineering students of Data Science, batch of 2022-2026 at Jain (Deemed-to-be University), Bangalore. As an educator, there is no greater joy than to witness the growth and development of one's students, and to see their creative abilities come to fruition. This collection showcases the creativity, imagination, and enthusiasm of each individual contributor, and serves as a testament to their dedication to the art of poetry.

The poems within these pages represent a diverse range of themes and styles, reflecting the unique perspectives and experiences of each contributor. From reflections on personal growth and self-discovery, to explorations of the world around us, these poems are a testament to the depth of thought and feeling that young minds are capable of.

As an editor, it has been an incredible journey to work with the students, and to help bring their poems to life. I believe that this collection represents the very best of what poetry can be, and I am honored to have played a role in inspiring them to explore their emotions and perspectives.

**Dr. Raisun Mathew**
Assistant Professor of English
Jain (Deemed-to-be University)
Bangalore, Karnataka, India

# Acknowledgements

*Sincere thanks to,*

Notion Press

---

Faculty of Engineering and Technology
Jain (Deemed-to-be University)
Bangalore, Karnataka, India

---

# 1

# Fights

**SKANDA HARVE**

**************************************************

Fights with friends are always cool,
Not in playgroups, but in school.
It was interrupted by the bell,
And, it was a great tale to tell.

When I grew mature enough,
I learnt fights aren't cool.
They hold grudges till the end of time,
Like parents in children's mime.

Now, child keep in mind,
Grandpa, at your age wasn't so kind.
I took fights throughout my childhood,
Trust me, it doesn't feel that good!

# 2

# The Green War

**MIRIAM MUTHONI MWANIKI**

*****************************************************

Here I stand and watch in massive pain
The grotesque condition of my slaughtered kin,
Now morphed to new shapes, would they say
And for them I can only pray!

Several men armed to teeth with powerful saws,
Instantly forcing my brothers on their knees,
These men then torture them to submission,
To different new shapes, my brothers emerge.

All of this their comfy houses to build,
Limbs of my brothers as firewood they're used,
And for the ones that resist submitting,
To black charcoal they are burnt!

As I watch them shed pain tears,
Echoes of their screams ringing in my ears,
And I uselessly rooted to the ground,
Can only think of ways to turn this around!

To finally avenge my wiped out clan,
The angry ancestors come up with a plan,
No more rain for this wicked man!
And for the shed blood rivers dry up.

# 3

# Mused in Thoughts

**ANVESHA BHUKTA**

**ANVESHA BHUKTA**

One fine calm night of many dreams,
I planned to sleep like a log
But my head had other plans to keep.

Bucket of memories deep in the well,
Bring it up or just being there to dwell.

Pondering my decisions I try to relax,
But the more I cry to try
I felt my brain getting waxed.

Although it seems a little dramatic
Trust me when I say, it feels more than it is.

This is me who muse on anything and everything around
And I try to cry though everything else in my mind is so loud.

# 4

# In Love

**SAATHWIKH GARGESH K.**

*****************************************************

Does it need any reason?
Will it need any season?
To enter into love,
Like a beautiful dove.

Does it have a language?
Could it be filled in a baggage?
Will there be more excuses or kisses?
We just call it limitless love.

She knows how I feel
Also knows how to heal.
Love can neither be defined,
Nor be denied.

How can you lose it
When you already cemented it.
There is no space for 'never',
It only has 'forever' and 'ever'.

# 5

# The Blue Sky

**LINGA JASWANTH**

******************************************************

The sky is blue
The clouds are white
Rain makes the sky dark
Storms make it brighter.

The clouds are like cotton
Spreading its wings
Free to fly in the sky
Like the wandering thoughts in me.

It's great again.
The thunder roars with might
Lightning strikes with its bright light
The storm passes, all is still
Leaving behind a rainbow on the hill.

Wind play with the clouds
Little clouds come together
It makes them the rain,
The feeling of smell from the rain is WOW!

# 6

# Verdant Nature

**SINGAMSETTY ROSHIK**

*****************************************************

It was my tender age,
Fall roll up to the 'winter tide'.
Accustomed life falling back to class,
With half crabby at stupid o'clock.

I relish ambient allurement,
Verdant bushes with water droplets.
The scenic is as 'pretty as a picture',
When I see through my class window.

All of a sudden I was caught on,
My name screaming loudly.
My teacher revile me for
I don't take notice him.

Even though I am not 'down in the dumps'
I feel like 'a shrinking violet'.
At last the verdant nature,
Of shrubs gratify my mind.

# 7

# One Heart

**JAMPULA KOUSHIK**

*******************************************************

Forget, but never regret!
Not everyone deserves another chance
To make a home in your heart.

Do it! We aren't here for so long.
Your voice is what I want to hear in throng
Spend time with me in my heart and sing a song
Let's make memories that will last a lifetime strong.

Embrace the pain, it shapes who we are
It teaches us to love, to reach for the stars
The memories we make, will never depart
Our hearts will hold on, forever, a work of art.

Infactuation isn't love, silence isn't anger,
Tears aren't weakness.
So set your heart a blaze.

Life is hard, so make your heart hard.
Even from ages, our emotions never change.

# 8

# The Passing Time

**DARSI DINAKAR YADAV**

****************************************************

Time is Chi-Chi costly,
Days are rolling quickly,
Everyday gives a new challenge,
Day by day I am stepping towards courage.

I want to learn how to grow,
It is messy every day, what to do?
I want to take out my Cozy,
I am wasting life with insensibility.

I want to cherish every moment,
Every sunrise, every sunset,
To live a life that is well spent,
And leave a legacy that won't end.

I want to face my fears, head on
To not let the clock beat me, and be gone
I want to make each day count,
And live a life that I can shout about.

# 9

# Sunlight

**LINGAM RAGHAVENDRA**

****************************************************

Sunlight, a gift from above
Brighter than a diamond, full of love
A blessing sent from the sky so blue
A light that will always shine true.

Sunlight, in the morning
When I woke up and open the window
The rays fall on me warming my skin,
It's a good delight and vibe.

Sunlight, blessing from above
A reminder of power of love
To brighten our lives, chase away the cloud
And bring joy to our hearts.

It's in the air, it's in the sea
It spreads its light and love
It brings us life, it makes the sight
A never ending golden shower of glee.

# 10 Sleepless Nights

**RAHUL BIKRAM NEUPANE**

****************************************************

Every night, I try to fall asleep,
Instead, I fall into a pit of despair.
Thinking of thoughts so deep,
All this boredom I can't bear.

The last time I had a pleasant dream
I can't quite remember it anymore.
I get these scary nightmares,
And they make me surrender for long.

In the morning, I feel so tired,
So much lazy and undesired.
All I wish for is to fall asleep,
Into the land of dreams I want to leap.

# 11

# The Edge of Seventeen

**DEVA VARSHINI K.**

*****************************************************

Been a kid, don't want to get rid.
Don't forget to be kind
At the same time
You want to sharpen your mind.

There are some days you get lost
But darling, get back to reality fast
Never lose your self-respect at any cost.

I know this age is peculiar
There is a haste in every venture
There are some things which will create magic.

Oh! I know it's really fantastic
Sometimes, I'll be standing motionless
With a huge surprise element in my face!

Dance in the rain, sing in the shower
Dive in the ocean, fly in the sky.

It's the best stage
Come out of your cage
Sometimes you will be mad
But you don't have to feel sad.

Felt like I am sick and down
Sometimes been a lonely clown
Learning from mistakes I made
I didn't literally fade.

When I look back all I feel is
Oh damn! Life isn't that easy at all, is it?

# 12

# I Wish I was Still Five

KANISH SHANMUGA R.

*****************************************************

I wish I was still five,
To know everyone, how I knew
Knowing my whole life was a lie
I'm restraining tears that are due.

My recollections, falling apart
I wish to forget, to move on
Yet it breaks my heart
So I hope for a new dawn.

I want to go, back in time
To when life was just a bliss
My reminiscence covered with grime
This feels like an abyss.

I'd like to get out of this nightmare
As I wish for it, not to thrive
But now none seems to care
I wish I was still five!

# 13

# Our Nature

**PRINCE KUMAR GUPTA**

****************************************************

Beauty speaks with feelings
Makes me lost in the lap of nature
No wondering where the world is diverging
Heal the soul while sleeping in the womb of mother.

Hearts feels no love under the sky anymore
Mother's womb is closed for many souls
Nature is crying alone in this world
Still the beauty of souls is not superior than money.

Wondering about nature under the tree,
Rebound me to my childhood
Nature was at its peak
Tears come to my eyes
Oh God ! Please heal the soul.

# 14

# It takes Courage to be a Coward

**NISHANT TIWARY**

*****************************************************

The morning after I killed myself,
I noticed the sun did not fail to rise again
But the pheonix did fail to rise back from it's ashes.

The morning after I killed myself,
I could not sense my heartbeat.
But I felt my mother's heartbeat running fast.

The morning after I killed myself,
I did not see the wind changing its direction.
But I regretted as I saw my parent's life had changed.

The morning after I killed myself,
Time had stopped for me.
But I could see the world running
As the watch did not stop for them.

The morning I killed myself,

The sun didn't fail to set with my downfall.

The morning I killed myself,
I woke up and put some sense to my brain

# 15

# The Kid

**NIKHIL CH**

*****************************************************

When I was a kid
I was not the one to think
About anything
Whether I play, eat, or drink.

When I was a kid
I used to be with my mother
I found her to be my world
She never left me in any situation.

But when I grew old
The love she showered to the child in me
Wasn't expressed back to her by me
Still the love had it natural flow from her onto me.

Can you give back the love
Your mother gives you for all the time?
You don't give back the love what you have got all the time.
Unconditional and irrevocable!

# 16

# As Long as You Love

**VISHAL V**

*****************************************************

Forests are blessings from the God,
We must be thankful to the Lord.
Animals explore them round and round,
But humans sell them for pounds and pounds.

We must show a bit of gratitude,
And throw away the nasty attitude,
This is the soulful life that we belong to
Travel with this life for long.

Longing for the life that we love
Spend your time with your beloved
Close your eyes and think about yourself
Make yourself proud as long as you love.

# 17

# Glimpse of Youth

SNEHA CHHETRI

**************************************************

When I was young and carefree,
I had nothing to worry or fear.
But as I grew older,
The weight of pressure broke my shoulder.

The peace and happiness of youth has flown,
Money brings happiness, they say.
Spent recklessly, not realizing its worth,
This journey of youth can be painful.

Some fight for their happiness till the end,
But if given the chance, I'd choose a different road.
Away from the mindless world, I'd escape,
To my own fictional world, I'd hold tight.

Is it too much to dream to live in our fiction?

# 18

# Sad Truth

**GANESH REDDY VAKAMALLA**

***************************************************

I don't know why,
People started fearing friends
Who used to be same strangers
Strangers being seen as aliens!

I don't know why,
When bonding becomes a rare piece
Everyone loses their peace.

I don't know,
Whether to choose friends or truth
When lies overcome the truth.

Sitting in the world of confusion
Unable to figure out a conclusion.

# 19

# Secret Crush

**K. P. CHANDRA SEKARAN**

****************************************************

You are not just my secret crush
But one of the reasons I simile.
Your birthday makes my heart as happy
As your presence in me.

You mean a lot to me that you would ever know
Priceless and inevitable dream of mine.

There's is nothing about you that I don't adore
You brighten up my life
Makes me feel happy to be alive.

Today, you shine brighter than the stars above,
You hold a special place in my heart,
May your birthday be filled with beauty,
Just like you are to me, a magnificent work of art.

# 20

# In My Head

**DINAH JIJU GEORGE**

*****************************************************

Surrounded, yet so alone
A fake smile is all I've known
Felt so judged for my scars
Not just the ones on my arm.

When did life get so complicated?
It used to be simple, till we got intoxicated.
Never anticipated my life this way
Having people, but not anyone who would stay.

I just want a break from the storm
The one I made on my own.
Please save me from the storm
Of having no one to call my own!

# 21

# The Dark

**M. SAI KARTHIK**

*****************************************************

Darkness creeps, hiding the light
A place where shadows and fear fight
A void that seems to have no tent and end.

Everyone's afraid of the darkness
But it can be peaceful and calm
A moment of rest.

Darkness can also be a warning sign
A call to action, to shed light
To fight the demons that brought us tears
In facing our fears, we find the way
To the brighter tomorrow.

So, embrace the dark and do not hide
That shows the true strength that resides.

# 22

# Guess Me

**DHARSHINY S. P.**

****************************************************

Hey, You Beauty! Why are you sad? I'm there
From your birth till death, I'm there.
Hearing you cry, I never smiled
Seeing you smile, I never cried.

The first day you fell, I too fell with you
The next day you laughed, I too laughed with you.

Never worry about failing alone, I have always failed with you
When you got betrayed, I was also betrayed
But trust me I'll never cheat you.

Remember, when you loved yourself I loved you too
But when you hated yourself I hated you too.

Pure and true once again, I'm there.
Couldn't guess who I am?
Yeah, I'm your shadow!

# 23

# Unfair

**AAVANI K. S.**

****************************************************

Why is life so unfair?
Challenging us to lots of dare
God, what do you gain
By making us suffer in pain?

Tears falling down like a rain
When everything goes down in vain.
God, Don't you care?
Why do you have to make it unfair?

Still we keep fighting again
Even if our dreams go down in the drain.
We'll fight even when life is unfair
And will keep fighting till its fair.

# 24

# Rain! Oh Mighty Rain

**MOHAMMAD MOHSIN**
****************************************************

What a rainy season it is
Pouring heavily for days.
Water, water, everywhere
Not a little sign of cease for a repair.

Stopped raining after a day
But flood came anyway.
Got stuck on the roof
Due to the blockage, aloof.

No sign of rescue anywhere
Shortage of food and supplies everywhere.
Lost the hope to survive,
Thought of ending my life.

But suddenly got the hopes to survive,
Soon came the rescuers of my life.
Thanked the God for the drive,
Wonder! What an experience of life it was.

# 25

# Rise

**S. HARSHAVARDHAN**

*****************************************************

I will rise
Over the wall.
I will rise and shine
Whenever I fall.

Like the sun,
That never dies.
And it comes in the early morning,
Every day it does rise.

After falling once,
Twice and thrice,
Again and again
I will rise and shine.

I will rise
After every fall,
And whenever I fall,
I will rise again.

# 26

# Dear Brother

**THARUN CHINTHA**

****************************************************

God has blessed me with a lovely brother
I'm glad to have that power.

When I'm feeling low, he makes me to glow
He comes and make me flow
Hope is in you, dear brother.

Be mine forever until we leave each other.
No matters what life throws at me
He'll always be there for me.

Though we are separated by distance,
Our bond is unbreakable, always persistent.

He guides me, scolds me,
And stands by me when others try to fold me.
He cares me like a mother
Loves like a father
Worries like a sister,
Love you, my dear brother.

# 27

# Mobile Phone

**KHUWAISH GOYAL**

****************************************************

One day, I fuelled my phone
And it came to life on its own.
It became my closest friend,
One I can't imagine living without.

One day, I shattered my heart,
I felt so sad, my life fell apart.
Days passed by, I had nothing to do,
Until the repair, and then, it all came through.

One day, the phone was fixed,
And happiness returned, my life was mixed.
Life became busy once again,
And in today's world, it's a vital part of our life's plan.

# 28

# Trip to Ooty

**B. HARSHA RATHAN**

*****************************************************

It was a summer season
I came upon the "Queen of Hills"
Positioned in the Nilagiri hills
The clouds lure and swing.

The romantic hills, dazzling
Climate, clustered carrots and so on.
Carrot gardens laid awning
Of tackful in mountains.

I felt serene on the peak
Unwilted breeze, hesitant heights,
Birds fluttering in the air.
The romantic tears fall on the mountains.

# 29

# The Mirror

**MIDDE CHARMISRI**

*****************************************************

What you see in me is not you,
There is someone else inside you.
You have everything hidden inside,
But everything seems perfect outside.

Your reflection may have a smile,
But your soul may cry hard.
You may see the outer beauty in me,
But your inner beauty might be suffering.

What you show to the world in me is false,
But what you experience in the crowd is true.
You can exhibit your emotions in me,
But you cannot be consoled by me.

You might be the strongest person,
But I know you well,
As I am the place where your reflection falls.

# 30

# Magnificent Mother Nature

**K. OMESH NAIDU**

************************************************************

Nature is everywhere
Everything lives and grows is nature.
It's the beauty spread all the way
Filled with dazzling knowledge and wisdom.

Spending time amidst nature's beauty,
Gaining insight, so precious and true.
Nature holds the essentials of life,
Bringing happiness, free from all strife.

Nature is a reality like no other,
A teacher of wisdom, like a wise mother.
For without nature, there can be no future,
We must keep it pristine, now and forever.

# 31

# The Search for a Cloud

**MEBIN RAJAN THOMAS**

****************************************************

I'm a nelophile,
Who fell in love with clouds.
One of those clouds,
Blocked the light of my life.

Another cloud, rained itself down
To bring the light back to my life.
She fell as a raindrop
Joined the river and then the sea.

I seek her in every drop.
Did she float away or dry up?
Has she joined the clouds again?
I wait for her to rain, forever.

# 32

# The Unforgiving Passage of Time

**PAWAN PANDEY**

*****************************************************

The night never waits
How tougher the life gets
Life's never been easy
Neither for you, nor for me.

Days and days running so fast,
Nothing would bother
Where you were
And where I was
The time bids good bye.

Offering red rose, the time goes away
Teaching us a lesson, we get nothing.

How long we may run, the time is so cruel
Looks not behind at any cost
Both of us are tied in an iron sack.

# 33

# To My Mother

**EASHA DAYANAND**




Thanks to my mother
One like no other
For making me tougher
And pushing me further.

The moments that we share
And the more that you care
I see no one better
Am I a debtor?

Now I see time ticking
And epiphany kicking
As I see this isn't forever
But I persist however.

# 34

# First Love

SYED ASHFAQ

*****************************************************

Deep and true is my love for you
It's a feeling I can't escape or subdue
I think of every blooming flower
And dream you every sleeping hour.

I can't forget you
Because I'm obsessed with you
I'll cherish every moment we share
And keep your love forever in my heart.

Thought you may never be mine
The moment we share will forever shine.

**SUDIPTA RAJ WAGLE**

****************************************************

The sun never shone as bright as today
The birds chirped as if there was no tomorrow
That smile, that smirk of yours all eat up my sorrow
A bright light, that shows me more contrast to life than I know.

The more I know you, the more I find in you
The lost, broken child that turned into a maiden
Those chains of trauma that grows within you
Worry no more girl, I'll make sure your heart ain't laden.

You've been through so much, but you still stand so tall,
And I admire the strength and courage, within you, enthralled.
I'll be here for you always, to hold your hand and guide,
And together, we'll face anything, with love by our side.

# 36

# The Lipstick on Lips

**MULAKALEDU SREE DHRUTHI**

****************************************************

Lipstick, oh lipstick,
A touch of color on your lips,
A burst of confidence, a hint of flair,
A simple swipe and you're ready to bear.

It's more than just a cosmetic tool,
It's a statement, a power move,
A splash of red, a pop of pink,
It lifts your spirit, it makes you think.

It's a symbol of femininity,
A tool of self-expression, a true rarity,
It's a powerful weapon, a way to shine,
A confidence booster, it's truly divine.

Lipstick, oh lipstick,
A small item with a big impact,
It transforms you, it lifts you high,
A little luxury that's worth a try.

# 37

# Friendship for Life

**THIRUMALESH K.**

*****************************************************

In a moment of weakness
If you can't stand on your feet,
A friendship for life
Is all what you need.

If you're stumbling through darknes
And you're searching for lead,
A friendship for life
Is all what you need.

If the sun burns like fire
And you can't stand the heat,
A friendship for life
Is all what you need.

If your life breaks into pieces
Cause devil's sowing the seed,
A friendship for life
Is all what you need.

# 38

# The Moon

**S. DEEPTHI REDDY**

*****************************************************

I'm sitting on the couch
Looking at the moon
I'm certainly not a werewolf
But I love the moon.

I love its colours
I love the starry sky
I love to look at them
Wherever I am.

The moon fascinates me
I wondered
It's right in front of me
Alone and unreachable.

# 39

# The Root of Life

**ABIN MUHAMMED**

*****************************************************

Nature is where we belong
From birth to death so long.
It's the sunshine and wind
That keeps us going like the water
In the sea and river, flowing.

The place where sorrows and joy melt,
Also where peace and patience is felt
It shows us the beauty of the world
As problems and concerns are burned.

Sometimes we forget everything
And tries to destroy the whole 'shebang'.
But we don't realise we are losing
Something without we can't live.

# 40

# The Joy of Life

**MUHAMMED SAJAL**

*****************************************************

Happy is life
Glowing like the sky
Delighted like I wanted
Smiling as I thrive.

I wanna be the sky
To grow up so high
To be the symbol of the success
To be vast positive till I'm alive.

Thrilled like I want
To be the reason for my own happiness
Making life's journey worth while.

# 41

# The Cricket World

**R. TEJA**

*****************************************************

Cricket is a game of joy,
A game that both boys and girls can enjoy.
With a rich history, it still shines
A sport that brings hope all over time.

It's filled with excitement and thrilling fun,
Teaching teamwork and valuable skills, one by one.
Our hearts filled with cheer, we cheer and shout,
In this game, we all join hands to play the game.

Cricket is a bond that brings us together,
A love for the game that lasts forever.
It's a treasure that we all hold dear,
A sport that we all hold dear, without any fear, forever.

# 42

# Untangling Depression

**ALURU SAHITHYA**

*****************************************************

Depression isn't a thing to be joked,
It's a demon that is provoked
It's a kind of disease,
Which leaves you in no ease.

You suffer from inside,
Hesitate to seek help from outside.
You hide the hurt, hide the pain,
You hide your tears that fall like rain.

Loneliness consumes you,
It eats away your years
Until your life is consumed by
The never ending fears.

But remember one thing.
You will be happy one day
Killing the demon on your way.
All you need to do is fight,
For one more night.

# 43

# Playground

**DEVALAMKATI SANJAY**

*****************************************************

Children play in the ground
Sun above their head
Sometimes they feel thirsty
Get busy in searching water.

Old age pensioners chitchat
They are bored in their house.
Kids run and have fun
Some are busy eating snacks.

It's always a special place,
Filled with cherished memories to embrace.
It's a sanctuary for the young at heart,
Where stress is released and memories start.

# 44

# Violet's Mystery

**SUMIT VARDHAN SINGH**

****************************************************

Violet, a hue so rich and true
A color that captures the heart's view.
A mystery, a blend of blue and red
A shade that both soothes and wakes the dead.

From the depths of the night sky to the first light,
Violet shows its face with all its might.
A symbol of royalty, a hue of grace
It's a color that leaves a lasting trace.

In a field of flowers, it stands alone,
A hue that's deeper, richer than we've known.
With a richness that draws the eye,
Violet is a color that never dies.

It's a color of passion, of love and peace,
A color that never seems to cease.
Violet is the color of the soul,
A shade that makes one feel whole.

So let us celebrate this hue so rare,
And all the magic that it can share.
For Violet, with its mystery and might,
Is a color that brings beauty to sight.

# 45

# The Darkest Days

**SUDHANSU KUMAR**

****************************************************

Going through the darkest days
Watching them winning the race
Hopes become high that a day will come
For me as well, to shine before them.

Shatter the chains of adversity,
Leave behind those who bring you pain.
Embrace your gifts, use them to flourish,
And create a better future for you to gain.

Walk away from the cruellest people on earth
Use your simile to change the world
And I wish a day will come
For you, to find the best in you to win the chase.

# 46

# Flower

## SIRISHA AGRAWAL

*****************************************************

Flower grows, strong and independent
Doesn't hold onto any men
Defies all the rules of conservative society
Radiates itself with a different feminity.

Petals, so soft yet witty and mighty,
Consists the power to break free
From this patriarchal society.
Goes through indefinite number of challenges,
Yet stands strong with all the vigilance.

Fragrance of a flower, so strong, so influential
It ignites the idea of gratitude and existentialism.
Always shines brighter and brightest
In the dazzling sunlight.

Feminism is a flower that spreads across
Miles and miles worldwide.

# 47

# Worth of Failure

**S. MURALI MOHAN REDDY**

*****************************************************

If I made a mistake
Then I would have to retake
And do it once again
Even I feel the pain.

But there also lies a prize
That made me realize
Even if I was to fail,
It would be a learning trail.

If I hope for medals beyond luck
I can't just rely on it alone
I must do hard work
To show the world my worth.

# 48

# The Red Rose

**POCHA SAI SURYA GANESH REDDY**

*****************************************************

Roses so delicate and divine,
Their beauty divine and sublime,
Their petals so gentle and soft,
Their colors that never aloft.

Their sweet aroma so divine,
Their sight that pleases my eyes,
Their thorns that protect their heart,
The beauty and power of its art.

The red roses of my life
Won't you touch me from your heart?
Make me feel your sweetest core
I may be hurt, still it's a lot to explore.

Roses, let it be mine
Althought it may sometimes bleed
The hope it spread smell so high
That I may live more for another try.

# 49

# In the Streets of Lahore

**PRERNA KUMARI**

*****************************************************

In the streets of Lahore,
Where every passerby
Carries along a beautiful part
Of the city, wherever they go.

In the streets of Lahore,
Where the air is moist with the warmth
Of the spicy hot bhajis.

In the streets of Lahore,
Where glances are the sweetest and
Purest when exchanged with the unknowns.

In the streets of Lahore,
Where the dusty lanes are covered
With the never-ending auto wallas and rickshaws.

In the streets of Anarkali Bazar
Which flocks with the finest
Of the finest ladies of Lahore,

In the streets of Lahore,
Where the city is filled with the sweetest talks
Of lovers in the evening park,

In the streets of Lahore,
Where the parks and gardens make the most of its glorious,
Magnificent piece of Art and History,

This is that city which will always be a part of my soul.
It's the beautiful city that I crave to be a part of,
Where my root lies, now a border away,
While I write this with a
A drop of tear in my book.

# 50

# I Shall

**RAISUN MATHEW**

****************************************************

I shall speak
Not to the walls, not to the chairs, not to the floors
But to the many souls of this nature
Dreaming the heights they could gain.

I shall listen
Not the crowd, not the rumours, not the spoilers
But the many voices around me
Hoping for a better reply than the other.

I shall read
Not the files, not the grades, not the letters
But the best hearts that beat for wisdom
Aspiring to have read by someone in the world.

I shall write
Not with ink, not for power, not the splendour
But with the finest notion of their words
Believing to have it read a million times.

I shall live
Not for dates, not for praise, not for race
But to be the best in their hearts for long
As a lovely thought that will never die down the road.

Printed by Libri Plureos GmbH in Hamburg, Germany